waste
want not

Contents

GW00419256

Publishers Disclaimer

The uses, hints, tips and ideas contained in this book are passed on in good faith but the publisher cannot be held responsible for any adverse results.

Why 'Waste Not Want Not'?

Millions of tonnes of household waste are produced every year and the majority is land filled rather than recycled or composted. But much of this waste is not rubbish at all and is simple to recycle or turn into new products.

We are all aware that we should be recycling, reusing and repackaging to save the environment and yet there is still a great deal more we can to do. We need to increase our recycling rates and reduce the amount of product which ends up in landfill.

There are lots of reasons to reduce and recycle your waste.

Landfill is harmful to the environment and expensive. As available space for landfill runs out the cost for more space rises.

Many of the items thrown into landfill are made from products that are slowly running out or may not be replaced so quickly or easily in the future. If we use this 'waste' again we can save space in landfill sites and reduce the need to mine new raw materials which can damage the surrounding environment.

Many items in landfill, such as glass, will never decompose. And yet, glass is a product which can be recycled indefinitely.

The use of plastic is growing every year and plastic takes hundreds of years to decompose.

The amount of packaging which is thrown away is frightening. A large percentage of your money goes on the new packaging which surrounds your new product, and this packaging ends up in the dustbin almost immediately. It is best to choose items which have minimal packaging but if you do find yourself with an item you know will not decompose easily it is time to think 'waste not want not'!

In addition to reducing product waste, we can also restrict our energy wastage. We all contribute to global warming when we heat our houses or use more water than necessary. Check out our easy tips to reduce the amount of energy you use which in turn will reduce the amount of money you spend on your utility bills.

Just following a few of the handy hints and tips in this book will help make a big difference to the environment. A few simple changes to our lifestyles can contribute to keeping the environment safe; reusing household items can save you shopping time, money and help save the planet!

Split into simple easy to follow sections covering paper, plastics, ceramics, glass, tin, textiles, food waste and energy, this book will aid you in making the most of the products you already own. From practical solutions to gift ideas this book will get you reusing and remaking!

And remember, many charities rely on reusing and recycling products to raise money. Help charities by contributing items you really cannot reuse. Always ask yourself whether your 'waste' should end up in landfill.

Paper and Card

Paper and Cardboard

In addition to regular recycling of paper and cardboard waste in the home, there are a number of things that you can do with old paper products to reuse them.

Cards

Gift tags
You can create gift tags by simply re-using the front of birthday or christmas cards that you have received. Cut a section from the card, whatever size and shape you like, then attach to the front of a gift with tape.

Cardboard Boxes

You are probably using cardboard boxes for storage somewhere in either your house, garage or shed but here are a couple of novel ideas you may not have thought of.

Dustcover
Simply cut the flaps from all 4 sides of a cardboard box to create a handy dust protector for small appliances, keyboards, laptops etc. You can leave as is or decorate with adhesive paper or paint.

Placemats
Cut to your desired shape and cover with adhesive paper or fabric. The beauty of using cardboard as placemat protectors is that you can create extra-large mats for large oven-to-table ware and when they are worn or dirty, simply make new ones!

Tray
Create a bespoke lap-tray by removing the flaps from the top of a cardboard box and then cutting an arch in two opposite sides which will fit snugly over your legs. Decorate the bottom of the box - which is now the top of the tray - with adhesive paper (washable is preferable in case of any spills).

Cereal Box

Magazine tidy
Create your own bespoke magazine tidy. Measure about 10cms up from one of the bottom corners of the box, and mark on the front of the box, draw a diagonal line from the mark to the top opposite corner of the box.

On the narrow side of the box draw a horizontal line from the mark across the width. From the end of the horizontal line, draw another diagonal line to the top opposite corner on the other wide side of the box.

Cut off the top section of the box following the lines you've drawn, then cover the box with paper or cloth of your choice to match your interior.

Egg Boxes/Egg Trays

Christmas ornament tidy
Keep glass and delicate christmas ornaments safe for another year by placing in egg boxes for storage.

Fire Starter
Fill each individual egg compartment with melted wax so that it is between one-quarter and one-half full then place a charcoal brickette in the wax.

If you are going to store this for future use, close the carton and place on a shelf. When you are ready to use, remove the top of the carton, and place the bottom half in the grill. Light the carton. Wait a few minutes and then add more charcoal. This will eliminate the need for lighter fluid.

Golf ball tidy
The base of egg boxes is great for storing golf balls!

Jewellery tidy/Little treasures storage
Keep small items of jewellery tidy by storing them in empty egg boxes. Cut the lid off the box and store in your bedside drawer. This is great for

storing earrings, brooches and the like. You can, of course, decorate the box - even colour coding each individual compartment for easy use.

Seed Tray

Egg boxes make perfect seed trays - simply fill each individual compartment with the compost/potting mixture and seed.

Juice /Milk Carton

Bird feeder

Cut an entrance hole into a juice carton half way down and remove the excess cardboard so that birds can easily get inside. Push a couple of twigs or bamboo skewers into the carton underneath the entrance which the birds can perch on.

Thread a length of twine or string through the top of the carton so that you can hang it from a tree. Then fill to just below the level of the entrance with bird seed.

Desk Tidy

Cut the juice carton about half way down and cover with material or paper of your choice to create a bespoke pen tidy for your home office.

Paint holder

For small paint jobs, cut the top of a carton and clean thoroughly then pour in your desired amount of paint, which will save you having to carry a large tin.

Kitchen Roll/Toilet Roll/Cardboard Tubes

Christmas light tidy

Wrap your christmas lights around a cardboard tube to keep them tangle free. Push the end with the plug inside one end of the tube and work your way along the length, wrapping the lights carefully and fixing with masking tape to stop from unravelling.

Crease free linens

If you would prefer your linens to be crease free, wrap around a tube after ironing and store in a kitchen drawer.

Crease free trousers and clothes

Prevent creases from forming on trousers or other articles of clothing hung over a hanger, by slicing a kitchen roll tube along one side and then pushing over the base or rack of the hanger. Stop ugly "hanger marks" appearing on the shoulders of woollens and other clothes by cutting two tubes along one side and then pushing onto each side of the hanger. These will act as a barrier against indentations caused by the hanger.

Drawer tidy

Cut the tubes into lengths of around 3-4 inches and put in your drawers to stop items getting muddled.

Extension cord tidy

This works better with a kitchen roll tube and works in two ways to ensure that your cables don't get all tangled up when you are not using them. You can either wrap the extension cord around the length of the tube then put the

"plug" end in the tube to secure it, or alternatively fold the extension cord back and forth in around 10 inch lengths and push inside the tube.

Fire starter "cracker"

Fill an empty roll with dried leaves in the autumn and then wrap the tube in newspaper, leaving about 4 inches at each end of the roll. Twist the ends of the paper, for easy lighting.

Nail Varnish Tidy

If you've got a drawer full of nail varnishes knocking against each other and you have to pull every one out before you get to the colour you like, try cutting tubes into lengths of around 3-4 inches. Mark the top of each piece with the colour from each bottle making it easier to identify the colour at a glance.

Paper and poster storage

Roll documents and posters tightly, and store in the tubes. Mark each tube with the contents for ease of reference.

Sapling protector

Slice a tube lengthways and place around the bottom of small trees to protect them whilst you are weeding around the area.

Seed planter

Cut into pieces around 3-4 inches in size and place in a tray. Half fill each tube with compost or potting mix and put a seed in each. When transferring the seeds, push the pieces into the ground around each seed to discourage worms and other pests.

Socks, stockings and tights storage

Fold socks, stockings and tights into the centre of tubes to keep them tidy and free from snags. This will keep them much tidier in your drawers and is also great if you are going on a trip for keeping hosiery easy to hand.

Newspaper

Newspaper, by design, is a very absorbent product, because it has to absorb ink. But that also means it is equipped to absorb all sorts of moisture.

Bird cage liner

Line the bottom of your bird cage with newspaper to make it easier to clean.

Coasters

Create your own coasters to protect surfaces by either folding or cutting sheets of old newspaper into a square. Tape the sides together to create stability and simply throw it away when it gets too stained.

Cobweb remover

Roll old newspapers together and secure around the middle and one end with an elastic band or tape. "Feather" the other end and use to remove cobwebs.

Deodorize food containers

Scrunch up old newspaper and fill containers to remove

lingering odours. You can also line the vegetable drawer in your fridge with newspaper to keep it dry and odour free. Refresh weekly, or more regularly in the case of spillage.

Frost Protection
Wrap fragile or small plants in newspaper in the winter months to protect from frost damage.

Kitty Litter Liner
Line the bottom of your cat's litter tray with shredded newspaper to help absorb odour.

Paper logs
Roll a few sheets of old newspapers together and stuff into the empty tubes left by toilet rolls or kitchen rolls and then use as an alternative or an addition to logs in your fireplace.

Protection from paint
When you're painting window frames or sills, wet old newspaper and completely cover the glass. Allow the paper to dry and this will act as a barrier and prevent paint getting onto the glass. When you have finished painting and the paint is dry, remove from the glass. Finish by cleaning your windows with the tip on the next page.

Ripen tomatoes
Wrap unripe tomatoes individually in newspaper and then leave at room temperature to ripen.

Shape maintainer
Scrunch up old newspapers and stuff into shoes, handbags and even hats when storing them to help maintain their shape.

Shoe dryer and deodorizer
If your shoes get soaked they can take ages to dry and develop a "mature" odour - but if you stuff your wet shoes with old newspaper, this will help them dry more quickly and absorb unpleasant pongs!

Stale odour remover

Scrunch-up old newspaper and place in suitcases for a couple of weeks to remove stale odours.

Table protector

Rather than go to the expense of buying one, create your own table protector by layering sheets of newspaper together and placing them underneath your tablecloth to act as a heat and moisture guard. You can secure the edges of the newspaper together with masking tape or decorators tape and when it is worn through, just make a new one! Much cheaper than having to re-varnish your table!

Window Cleaner

In a bucket, make a solution with equal parts water and white vinegar. Tear the old newspapers into A4 size sheets, crumple and then saturate in the cleaning solution. Squeeze any excess liquid from the newspaper then apply to your windows in a circular motion, replacing the newspaper as it begins to disintegrate. Wipe the window dry with a clean dry sheet of crumpled newspaper.

Weed suppressant

Layer newspaper around the base of your garden plants and soak with water. Spread mulch over the top and this will create a barrier to weeds, plus lock in moisture.

Wrapping

Wrap delicate items and ornaments in individual sheets of newspaper and store using crumpled newspaper to prevent damage. Do not use newspaper to store silverware.

Plastics

Plastics

The world's annual consumption of plastic materials has increased from around 5 million tonnes in the 1950s to nearly 100 million tonnes today, which means that we produce and use 20 times more plastic today than we did 50 years ago. In western Europe plastics consumption is growing about 4% every year.

Packaging represents 35% of UK plastics consumption which is the largest single sector use and plastic is the material of choice in nearly half of all packaged goods.

It is vitally important that whenever you can, you opt out of using plastic materials or choose wherever possible plastics that have been recycled. Choose goods with minimal packaging or in a material that can be returned to the store.

Try to reduce the need to throw away plastics. For example, take a reusable shopping bag to the supermarket or shop, or re-use the bags you were given last time. Don't accept a bag if you don't need one. Plastic waste, such as plastic bags, often becomes litter. A study in 2003 showed that nearly 57% of litter found on UK beaches was plastic.

When they are beyond reuse, plastic carrier bags can be put into collection banks at most major supermarkets and stores. Every year, an estimated $17\frac{1}{2}$ billion plastic bags are given away by supermarkets. This is equivalent to over 290 bags for every person in the UK.

If you have a surplus of clean useable carrier bags, try giving these to local second hand shops, libraries, markets or charity shops who will be grateful and will reuse them.

Bags

There are of course numerous household uses for carrier bags, so here are just a few.

Bathtoy collector

Hang a carrier from the taps of your bath to create storage for bath toys. Make a small hole in the bottom to allow water to drain and stop tops from going mouldy.

Biscuit basher

If your recipe needs broken biscuits, put them in a carrier bag and tie securely. Bash the bag against your work surface, or with a rolling pin, then simply untie the bag and empty into a bowl.

Boot waterproofs

Make sure that feet are kept dry in your boots or wellies. After you've put your socks on, put each foot in a carrier bag before you slip your boots on to give added waterproof protection. Alternatively, if your boots are wet when you need to put them on, put carrier bags over your feet to keep them dry.

Car tidy

Keep a handy carrier in your car to use as a bin on long trips to make sure your car doesn't end up full of rubbish.

Cracked Vase

If you have a favourite vase but it has a crack in it, place a carrier in the vase before you fill it with water which will stop any leaks.

Frost protector
If a cold night is predicted, place a carrier bag over the wing mirrors on your car and secure. In the morning your mirrors will be frost free.

Homemade manicure and pedicure
If your hands or feet are feeling dry and chapped, slather with petroleum jelly and place inside a plastic bag. Wrap a warm towel around the bag and leave for around 15 minutes which will rehydrate and soften the skin.

Litter tray liner
Line the bottom of your cat's litter tray with a carrier to make it easier to remove the used litter and clean.

Makeshift gloves
There are plenty of mucky jobs around the house - but you can keep dirt and grime off your hands by putting a carrier bag over each hand and using as "gloves". This also works if you hands are dirty and you need to touch something which is clean where you don't want to transfer the dirt.

Nappy Sacks
Don't waste money on store bought nappy sacks, simply reuse carrier bags to dispose of soiled nappies.

Paintbrush storage
Rather than clean paintbrushes when you are in the middle of a job and need to take a break, cover the brush with a carrier bag and secure around the handle with an elastic band. This way the paint will not dry on the brush and you can continue where you left of. This also works for paint rollers and paint trays.

Plant protector
As winter sets in protect your plants by cutting a small whole for ventilation in the bottom of a carrier then place the bag over the plant and weight down the handles with small rocks to stop the wind taking it.

Poop Bags

Be a responsible dog owner and carry bags with you when you are out walking to use to clean up after your pet. Take two bags - one to use as a "glove".

Ripen fruit

If your peaches or pears are rock hard, place them in a carrier bag with a ripe banana and leave for a day. The ripe fruit will release gases which will help soften the unripe fruit.

Salad spinner

Loosely wrap your washed lettuce in kitchen roll and then place in a carrier bag. Hold by the handles and spin the carrier bag quickly several times to remove the excess water.

Scrap collector

If you are having a group of family or friends over to dinner, make cleaning up easier by lining a large bowl with a carrier bag and scraping the plates straight into the bowl - this will save you having to make numerous trips to the bin. Once the bag is full tie up the handles and throw away.

Shoe and bag shaper

Scrunch up old carriers and stuff into shoes, handbags and even hats when storing them to help maintain their shape.

Stop paint splashes

Cover ceiling shades and wall lights with carrier bags when painting to protect from paint splashes. Make sure you do not switch on the lights when they are still covered.

Suitcase organiser

Use carrier bags to help organiser your suitcase by putting socks in one, swimwear in another etc. You may also like to wrap your liquids individually in carrier bags to protect your clothes from leaks. Alternatively, you could just pack your toiletry bag in a carrier to act as a barrier against leaks. Carrier bags are also good for keeping dirty or wet clothes away from the other clothes in your case.

Bottles

Recently there have been many rumours and questions regarding the health risks associated with reusing plastic bottles. While plastic water and soft drink bottles are sold with the intention of single use, then recycling, they can be safely reused if cleaned and handled properly. The key is to ensure that the bottle is not damaged, has been thoroughly cleaned before each use, and is filled with clean tap water.

The reuse of bottles has recently been discussed as having possible health risks. There are two main concerns. There is a potential for the presence and growth of bacteria in these bottles, but with proper cleaning and handling, this risk can be minimised.

Another health concern sometimes mentioned around the reuse of plastic bottles is that the plastic may breakdown and release 'chemicals' into the water. Current research into this topic indicates that these concerns are unfounded.

It is important to note that water or soft drink bottles shouldn't be shared during use - they should be used by one individual only to prevent the spread of germs that can lead to illnesses such as meningococcal disease.

Refilling water bottles can result in contamination of the water with bacteria, for example from the hands or mouth of the person filling or using it.

With time and in warm conditions, bacteria can multiply to harmful levels, but safe handling and proper cleaning can help prevent this from happening.

Recent reports have specifically suggested that a common plasticiser, DEHA, can leach from plastic soft drink bottles into the liquids they hold, particularly with reuse. However, the majority of plastic water and soft drink bottles are made with a substance called PET, and do not contain DEHA.

While current research indicates chemicals are not released into water by reuse, many of these bottles are manufactured to be recycled, not reused. Some plastic bottles can warp when exposed to heat in the cleaning process. It is therefore important to ensure that after the bottle has been washed in hot water and left to air dry that it is intact and has not been damaged.

Before filling bottles, wash and dry your hands thoroughly so that you don't contaminate it with bacteria. Examine the bottle to ensure that it is not damaged. After use, clean bottles and nozzles with hot, soapy water and make sure the inside of the bottle air dries completely before use.
Use good quality water from a safe source.

Bottles should be used by one individual only. Don't share bottles- saliva can transfer germs that can lead to illnesses such as meningococcal disease. Make sure they are labelled with the person's name for easy identification.

Again, there are of course numerous household uses for bottles, so here are just a few.

Cloche

Protect seedlings from cold or windy weather by using your empty plastic bottles to create cheap and effective cloches. In addition to protecting your plants from the elements, the bottles will also deter pests and wildlife and act as a barrier against insects and slugs.

Remove the cap and any labels from the bottle and using a serrated knife cut the bottom off the bottle. You can adapt the size of the cloche to suit your garden needs by making the cut closer to the top or the bottom, but remember you will need to push the cloche about an inch into the soil for maximum stability.

Desk Tidy

Cut a plastic bottle horizontally about halfway day and cover with decorative paper or fabric to create a handy desk tidy.

Door Stop

Fill a plastic bottle with stones to create a handy door stop. You can paint or decorate the bottle with fabric of your choice to complement your room design.

Drink Cooler

When the sun beats down and you are having a barbeque or party in the garden to ensure that you have lots of cold drinks try the following. Fill about a dozen plastic bottles with water and freeze them overnight. Put the frozen water bottles into a large bucket and add your drink cans or bottles.

The ice in the bottles will take longer to melt than if you just use normal ice cubes in the bucket and as the thawing ice is contained in the bottles it means that you can control the disposal of this, rather than have water slopping around in a bucket which could be a potential hazard.

Plastics

You can also freeze smaller plastic bottles and then use these in a rucksack or picnic basket to pack around foodstuffs and drinks to keep them cool.

Extension cord tidy

As with cardboard tubes, you can make a handy extension cord tidy using the "tube" of a plastic bottle.

Cut off the top and bottom to create a tube and you can either wrap the extension cord around the length of the tube then put the "plug" end in the tube to secure, or alternatively fold the extension cord back and forth in around 10 inch lengths and push inside the tube.

Piggy Bank

Decorate a bottle with paint or fabric of your choice. Cut a slit in the neck of the bottle, large enough to drop coins through. When the bank is full, cut around the bottom to release your coins.

Plant and seed starter

Cut a bottle in half and fill the bottom with potting compost or soil, add seed and water. Reattach the top of the bottle (with the cap on) using tape. Keep in a warm place and wait for the seeds to germinate.

Plant Waterer

Punch a few small holes in the cap of the water bottle, fill the bottle with water and put the cap back on. Turn the bottle over and bury in the soil of your hanging basket or pot plant. Another way of doing this is to remove the cap and cut off the bottom of the bottle. Turn the bottle upside down, and set the spout into the ground or pot. Fill with water and this will allow your plants to be watered when you are going to be away for a few days.

Potpourri Holder

Cut a plastic bottle horizontally so you end up with a cup or shallow dish as required. Decorate this new container with paints, paper or fabric of your choice. Fill this with potpourri and then cover the open end with a light material that will allow air to circulate but will contain the potpourri - such as netting, lace or muslin. Use an elastic band to secure the material in place and tie a decorative ribbon over the elastic.

When you need to refresh your potpourri, simply take off the ribbon and elastic band and refill.

String tidy
Keep string or wool from getting tangled. Cut off the bottom of a bottle and insert the string or wool, then pull a strand through the top of the bottle. Tape the bottom back on the bottle to keep the string inside and then when you need it simply pull the required amount through the top of the bottle - but make sure you always leave enough hanging so the end doesn't go back into the bottle.

Socks, stockings and tights storage
Cut the top and bottom from a bottle to create a tube then fold socks, stockings and tights into the centre of tube to keep them tidy. Make sure that you do not have any rough edges that could cause snags.

Containers

Many of the foods we buy these days come in plastic containers, whether they need them or not. Re-use the containers from ready meals or meat trays through your home and garden. Clean all containers thoroughly before you use them again.

Dog dish
Rinse clean a plastic container and keep it in the back of your car to create a portable water bowl.

Drawer tidy
Rinse clean a plastic container and use it to store odds and ends in your drawers. Great for storing cosmetics, nail varnishes or sewing materials.

Pest deterrent

Keep pests and slugs away from your flowers and vegetables by tempting them with a tasty treat. Dig a hole the size of the container and drop into the soil so that it is flush with ground level. Fill the container with beer to attract those pesky critters who will then fall in and meet their maker!

Seed Tray

Plastic containers make great seed trays - just wash thoroughly, fill with soil and plant seeds ready for germination.

Again, many of the foods that we buy have plastic lids - such as cream, custard, soups, pasta sauces etc. Here are a few ideas of how to reuse them. Wash thoroughly before reuse.

Coasters
Protect your surfaces by using lids as coasters, but be careful not to put anything too hot on them as this may cause the plastic to melt.

Craft palette
Use a clean lid to act as a mini palette when mixing paints or other materials to use in craft projects.

Drip Tray
Save your fridge from icky sticky drips by placing the lids under items to catch any drips.

Lid
I know it may seem obvious, but use any lids you have on half-used cans. They can be placed over the top to stop odours escaping or insects attacking!

Paintbrush drip guard
Make a small cut in the middle of the lid and push the handle of a paintbrush through so creating a "guard" to catch any drips of paint and stop them running down onto your fingers and hands.

Scraper
If you are trying to remove burnt-on food from a non-stick pan, try scraping gently with a plastic lid as this will be less abrasive then other cleaning tools.

Water Tray
Put lids underneath your house plants to act as a water tray, allowing plants to remain moist but your surfaces to be kept dry.

Plastics

Straws

Plant label/identifier

Use straws as markers in the garden. Write the name of what you have planted on a piece of paper, roll this up and insert it into a plastic drinking straw then push the straw into the ground near the plant.

Wrap/Cling film

Keyboard cover

If you are going away on holiday and know that you won't be using your keyboard for a week or two, cover it with cling film which will act as a dust protector.

Paint

You can keep stored paint in better condition and give it an added shelf life by covering the top of the paint tin with cling film before you put on the lid. Paint can be damaged by air getting into the tin, so an additional airtight barrier adds extra protection.

Paintbrush storage

As with plastic bags, if you need to take a break from a decorating job covering the brush with cling film will prevent the paint from drying out which means that you can then take up where you left off without having to laboriously clean brushes.

Remove hangnails

If you develop a hangnail you can remove it easily by applying handcream to the affected area and then wrapping the fingertip in cling film. You can secure the cling film with tape - but whilst it must be snug to make this work, do not make it so tight that it creates a circulation problem. The cling film will confine the moisture and soften the cuticle making it easy to get rid of the hangnail.

Ceramics, Glass & Tin

Tins/cans

We all try to use more fresh produce nowadays but we still use some things in tins!

Here are some interesting ways to reuse tin cans before you put them in the recycling bin.

Pet Food Scoop
Use as a scoop for your dried dog or cat food.

Outdoor Lanterns
Use tin cans for outdoor candles/lanterns. Get together a few tins and fill with water and freeze. (Freezing the water in the can enables you to hammer nails into the can to make holes without the can caving in.) When the water has frozen, take a nail and hammer holes into the can in any pattern you want. Let the ice melt and put tea lights or other small candles inside. The tin will glow through the holes for a really cool look. You could also paint the tins for extra effect.

Cookie cutters
You can use different size tins for cutting the cookies!

Protecting Plants
Cut the top and the bottom off the tins and place them in the soil. You can then plant your baby plants in them. This will help support them and also help to keep the slugs away.

Ceramics, Glass & Tin

Aluminium foil

Most people don't think about reusing aluminium foil, but it can be washed after you have used it the first time. Just wash in the sink and hang out to dry and you can use it all over again!!! Here are some interesting ways to use aluminium foil.

Cleaning your BBQ grill
Scrunch up a piece of foil and use to clean your grill, it cleans just as well as c wire scrub brush.

Funnel or Piping bag
Fold the foil to double thickness and roll into a cone shape. Cut off the end and you can now use it as a pouring funnel or you could fill it with icing and cut a much smaller hole, fold over the top and you have a piping bag.

Ironing Delicates
If you need to iron delicate fabrics such as silk or rayon, place a piece of foil on your ironing board and put the garment on the foil. Then pass 3 inches above the garment with the iron several times, holding down the steam button the whole time. The wet heat from the foil will get rid of the wrinkles!!

Preventing static from your dryer
You can prevent your clothes from having static electricity by throwing a small crumpled up ball of foil into your dryer.

Softening brown sugar
If brown sugar is left a while it sometimes goes hard. A way to soften it up again is to wrap it in foil and put it in the oven at about 150°C for 5 minutes. To keep it soft leave it wrapped in the foil and store it in a ziploc bag.

Sharpening Scissors
Layer about 8 pieces of foil and cut through them with your scissors - your scissors will now be sharp again!

Vegetable Pouches

An easy way to cook veggies on the BBQ is to put them onto a piece of foil and wrap them up into a little pouch. Put a little butter and a few of your favourite herbs inside the pouch to flavour the veggies before you close it.

Wrapping paper

It makes great wrapping paper and you can decorate it as you wish.

Wire coat hangers

Cloches

Make mini-cloches with discarded or broken wire coat hangers. Pull into a square shape. Place the hook in the soil and push down gently until the natural bend in the wire rests on top of the soil. Place another
a short distance away in your seed bed to create two ends of a cloche. Now throw over a sheet of plastic and hold down with logs or stones.
Note: this will work only when creating very small cloches.

Ceramics

Growing Herbs

Try growing herbs in broken mugs.

Handle-less cups

You could rub down the cup where the handles broke off and reuse them as handle-less cups.

Plant pot drainage

When you have really smashed a plate/bowl or mug the bits can make excellent drainage material for the bottom of plant pots - especially a curved piece put over any large hole to stop it getting clogged with earth but allow water through. It is quite fun to spot old cup pieces when you repot.

Ceramics, Glass & Tin

Plant Saucer

Broken plates can be used as saucers under plant pots to collect the water.

Paint pots.

Broken mugs are great for using as paint pots for crafts especially if you are using decent amounts of poster paints. You can give the paint a good slosh around inside without it splashing everywhere.

Pen Holder

If you have broken the handles off your favourite mug, how about using it as a pen holder on a desk. Just keep the handle-less side facing away

Soil

Since ceramics are totally inert, you could "recycle" them by breaking them up into bits as small as you can manage and then just mixing them into the soil in your garden. They'll do no more harm than all the other stones in there, although they may make the soil a little more alkaline than it was.

Glass

Glass Bottles and Jars

Glass bottles and jars are great for storing things in. Here are a few things you can use them for.

Bath Salts

Make your own bath salts and store in glass bottles. Here is a basic bath salt recipe for you to use.

250ml Epsom salts
10-20 drops fragrance oil
250ml cup sea salt
10 drops food colouring

Place the salts in a large bowl and mix well. Scoop out about 1/2 cup into a small bowl. Add the fragrance oil and food colouring to the salts in the small bowl and mix well. Add the blended mixture to the large bowl a little at a time until you are pleased with the colour strength.
Pour your salts into a glass bottle with a wide neck with a tight fitting lid.

Nails and Screws

Use glass jars to store all your screws and nails in. Then when you next need that particular nail, instead of scrabbling around in your tool-box, you will be able to find it a lot quicker.

Office/Sewing tidies

For a clean, fresh look, use clear jars (and glasses) of various heights and shapes to hold office or sewing supplies.

Salad Dressing

Glass jars are great for making and storing salad dressing. Put the oil, vinegar, lemon juice and seasoning into the jar, put the lid on and shake!!!

Wine bottles

Put candles in the top to make pretty table decorations.

Ceramics, Glass & Tin

Clothes and Textiles

Clothes and Textiles

Charity shops rely on our generous donations, so in the first instance, make sure any clothes or shoes that are still wearable are cleaned and donated to the charity of your choice.

In addition, most recycling centres now cater for textiles and shoes, so anything that you can't think of a secondary use for should be recycled. Remember that in general, most textiles make good cleaning rags but ensure that buttons, zips and other fastenings or fixings are removed before you use them. Textiles made solely of natural fibres (eg. cotton or wool) can also be added to your compost. Cut into small pieces, and add them gradually.

Blankets

Animal bedding
Re-use your old blankets as bedding for your dog and or cat.

Exercise mat
Fold a blanket into quarters and stitch the loose ends together to create an exercise mat

Boots and shoes

Garden containers.
Create a unique feature and alternative to shop bought containers by planting up your old shoes and boots. Make holes in the soles for irrigation and then plant up as with a standard container.

Tool storage
How about nailing an old pair of shoes to the wall of your garage or workshop and using these to store longhandled tools such as screwdrivers, hammers and paintbrushes.

Animal Bedding

Machine-washable jumpers past their prime make good cat/dog bed liners. There is no need to cut them up, just remove anything that may be a choking hazard.

Cushion Cover

Cut a jumper underneath the bust line to remove the arms and leave you with a woolen tube. Securely sew the bottom of the jumper with a zig-zag stitch and hem the cut end of the tube with wool removed from the discarded section. Make a fastening for the open end with either buttons, velcro or a zip - just remember if you cut the wool to hem it to stop from fraying. Place the cushion pad inside of your new snuggly cushion cover.

Fingerless gloves

If the elbow in your jumper is worn through, cut the sleeve off below the elbow then unravel and cut off about 6 of lines of wool. Next use some of the wool you have unravelled to hem the ends of the sleeve to stop it unravelling any further. Next cut a hole around 1 inch in width at the side of the sleeve about 3 inches from the cuff and then sew around this hole with the remaining wool to stop the hole from getting bigger.

Handwarmer

Using one sleeve from an old jumper, hem both ends with a zig-zag stitch to stop unravelling then use as a muff or handwarmer.

Hotwater bottle cover

Try creating a cover for your hotwater bottle. Cut the jumper into two rectangular pieces about 3 inches larger than the size of your hotwater bottle. Turn the rectangles so that you are working on what will be the insides of your cover then join together on 3 sides using zig-zag stitching to stop the wool from unravelling.

Create a hem around the open end by turning over about 1/2 inch and then thread ribbon through. Turn your cover the right way round and place your hotwater bottle inside, then tighten around the neck by pulling on the ribbon and tie securely. As always when using a hotwater bottle, use with care and be careful with boiling water.

Leg warmers

If the arms of your old jumper or cardigan are not worn through try making a pair of legwarmers. Create a hem around the larger end of the arm using a zig-zag stitch, ensuring the wool will not unravel and thread with loose elastic.

Make a new jumper!

Unravel the wool from an old jumper and make a new one.

Partner pillow

Take a pair of scissors and cut straight up the middle of an old jumper. Sew the cuff, bottom of the jumper and the edge that you have just cut with a zig-zag stitch to prevent fraying. Through the open neck stuff the jumper with padding - the other half of the jumper is a good place to start but any material remnants will work. Once the pillow has been stuffed, sew the neck area closed and you've created a snuggly partner pillow to cuddle up to.

Textiles

Snood

You can create a fabulous hood or snood using an old jumper. Cut the jumper underneath the bust line, removing the arms and leaving you with a woollen tube. Unravel some wool from the discarded section and use this to stitch the cut end of the woollen tube, to stop it from fraying or unravelling. Great for keeping out chills on a winter day!

Tea cosy

Cut the arms from a jumper and using the larger end, create a tea cosy. Sew the smaller end with zig-zag stitch to stop fraying and make a bobble for the top.

To make the bobble, cut two circles from card using the template in the last page of this section. Hold the templates together and tie the end of a ball of wool around both sections then thread the ball through the circles until they are completely covered and the gap in the centre of the templates has all but disappeared.

Then carefully snip the wool along the outer edge of the template, ensuring the templates are held together. Thread another piece of wool in between the two circles and pull together as tight as possible, then knot together. Remove the circle templates and fluff out your bobble. You can adapt the template to any size you need.

Pillowcases

Clothes protector

Keep dust and moths away from seasonal clothes by storing them in pillowcases. You can also cut a hole in the closed end of a pillowcase and then slip this over the top of your clothing whilst hung up, to protect from dust.

Duster

In common with most textiles, old pillowcases make great dusters and they can also help in those hard to reach places where cobwebs gather. Place a pillowcase over the end of a broom or mop to give you better access to ceilings.

Laundry Bag

Create bespoke laundry bags for all the family. Thread a cord through the top of a pillowcase to create a drawstring bag that can be hung on a peg or back of the door, and used to store your laundry until wash day. You can personalise the bags with names or categorise the bags, i.e whites, woollens, colours etc.

Napkins

Your pillowcases may be worn or stained in a particular area but there may be plenty of material that is still OK, so if this is the case cut squares from the pillowcases to make new napkins.

Storing Sheets

Keep spare linens neat and tidy by placing in a pillowcase before putting them in your cupboard. This is an easy way of creating more storage space in your cupboard and making sure that matching sets are kept together.

It also means you won't have sheets tumbling out on top of you if you need the sheet at the bottom of the cupboard! Unexpected overnight guests can also be catered for quickly as it will stop you searching through your linens for a matching set.

Travel Laundry Bag

Take a pillowcase away with you when you travel to keep your dirty laundry separate from

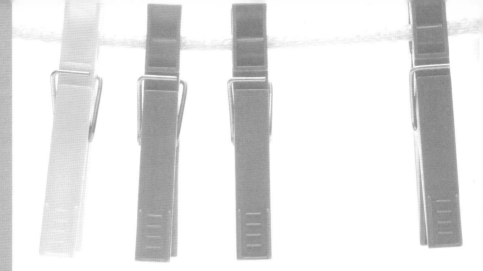

your clean clothes. This is a great tip if you are travelling to more than one destination when you have to re-pack your case. When you arrive home simply empty the pillowcase into your washing machine. Wash and dry the pillowcase and put back in your suitcase ready for your next trip.

Toy Sack

Create a fun toy sack for the younger members of the family - or create a Santa sack for Christmas! Using the templates at the back of this section, cut out the letters in different coloured and different textured remnants of fabric and stitch to the pillowcase. Thread a cord through the top of a pillowcase to create a drawstring bag to keep the toys neat and tidy.

Shirts and blouses

Peg Bag

Cut the sleeves from an old shirt or blouse and sew closed the holes. Sew along the bottom of the shirt (you can reduce the size) and hang on a wire hanger. Affix the shirt to the hanger by sewing along the arms of the hanger then hang on your washing line to keep your pegs to hand.

Shopping Bag

Cut the sleeves from an old shirt or blouse and sew closed the holes. Sew securely along the bottom of the shirt. Use the discarded sleeves to create the handles of the bag which is great for carrying fruits and vegetables.

Air freshener for your car

Cut a section from your stockings and tie one end. Place a handful of potpourri into the sachet and secure with ribbon which you can then tie around your rear view mirror.

Fishing Net

Create your own fishing net for the kids or for using in your garden pond for removing debris. Cut a section roughly 12 inches from the base of the toe and create a hem big enough to run a length of wire through. Push the wire through the hem and twist ends together.

Affix the wire to a broom handle or pole. Ensure that there are no sharp ends left on the wire, especially if you are giving the net to children to play with.

Flour duster

Cut a section of about 6 inches up from the toe of your stockings and fill with flour, then knot. Simply shake or knock the bag over the item that you wish to dust with flour.

Hair band

Cut a strip from your tights or stockings and wind this around your hair making a homemade scrunchie for your ponytail.

Head band

Keep your hair back from your face when applying beauty products by cutting a strip from your tights. Place your head through the strip (as if you are putting on a polo neck) and then pull the band slowly back up over your head until your hair is covered and pulled tight back off your face to your hairline.

Textiles

Lavender sachets

Create lavender sachets to keep your drawers and cupboards smelling sweet. Cut sections from your stockings and tie a handful of lavender buds into each.

Onion and garlic sack

You can give your onions and garlic extra shelf life by hanging them in tights or stockings to increase the air flow. Cut off a stocking or pair of tights at around knee level. Drop an onion into the bottom and tie a knot above the onion. Drop another onion into the stocking and again tie a knot above the onion. Repeat until you have each of your onion or garlic bulbs, tied into place and then hang in a cool, dry cupboard.

When you need to use an onion simply snip the stocking off underneath each knot so that you have easy access. It is also a great way of keeping track of how many onions or garlic bulbs you have so that you can buy more when you are running low.

Outdoor soap holder

Put a bar of soap in the toe of a stocking and tie to your outside tap. You can then wash your hands through the nylons which means no mucky handprints on door handles or dirt in the indoor sinks.

Perfect pastry

Perfect pastry is all about the consistency and gloopy sticky pastry is tough to remove from any rolling pin, so cover the rolling pin in a clean piece of stocking and then dust with flour before rolling your pastry. The stockings will hold enough flour to stop the pastry sticking to the rolling pin, and when you've finished you can either wash and reuse the stocking, or simply throw it away.

Plant bulbs

Tights and stockings make great storage sacks for bulbs as they allow the air to freely circulate. Cut your tights into the required size and knot both ends to keep the bulbs secure. Fix a label to your bulb sacks with the name of the plant for easy planting next season.

Plant ties

Cut strips from your tights or stockings and use these as ties in the garden to support saplings and climbing plants. The stretch in the fabric will allow the plants to grow without causing any damage, which can happen with more traditional wire based plant ties.

Shoe buffer

Use strips of old stockings to buff up your shoes after you've applied shoe polish.

Strain paint

Tights or stockings can be used as a homemade filter to remove any lumps from your paint. Take the lid off your paint tin and then pull a section of the stocking across the top and affix with an elastic band. Slowly and carefully tip the paint from the tin into a paint tray or paint bucket and you will have lump-free paint to help you get great results when decorating your home.

Trousers

Baby support pillow

Help support a baby while he or she works on learning how to sit up. Take a pair of trousers or jeans, cut the legs off to the desired length, sew across the bottom and stuff well with padding. The baby can sit in the crotch area to have just that little bit of extra support while learning to balance, and the legs will cushion any falls.

Draught excluder

Cut the leg off the trousers to your desired size and sew one end securely to make a tube. Stuff with material remnants (or old newspapers) and then either sew or tie off the other end. Put in front of doors to keep out chilly draughts.

Templates

To use the templates in this section, either trace with tracing paper, or place on a photocopier then fix to either cardboard or fabric as required. If you are using a photocopier you can increase or decrease the size of the template to fit your own needs.

Template for bobble

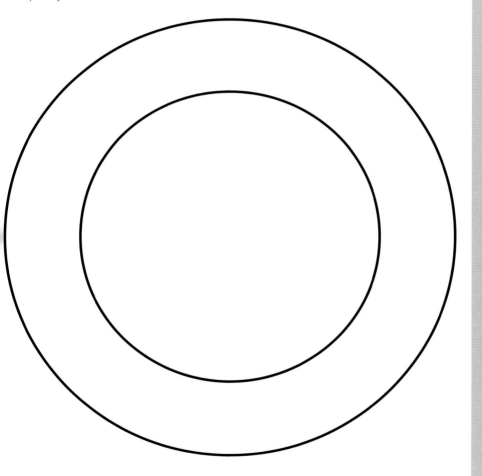

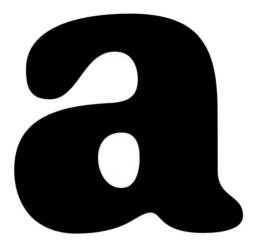

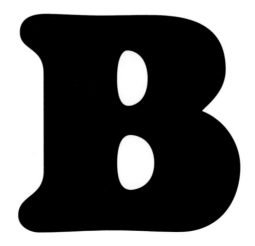

Template for Toy Sack

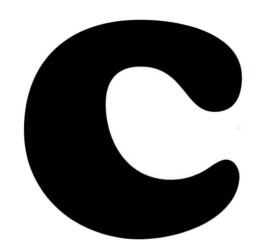

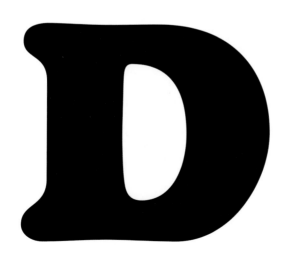

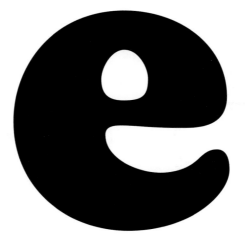

Template for Toy Sack

Template for Toy Sack

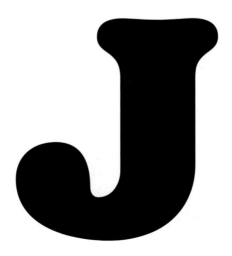

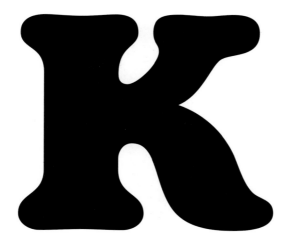

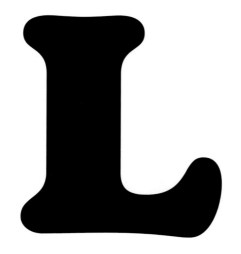

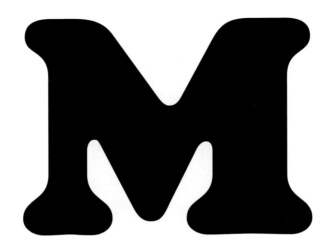

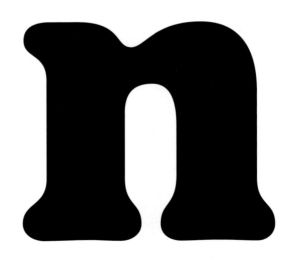

Template for Toy Sack

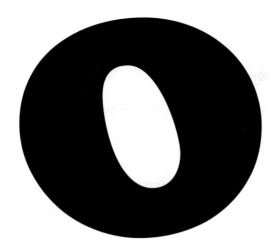

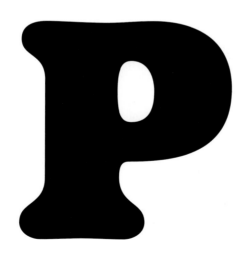

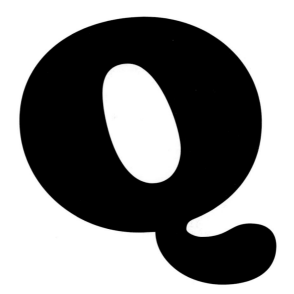

Template for Toy Sack

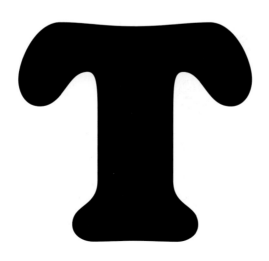

Textiles

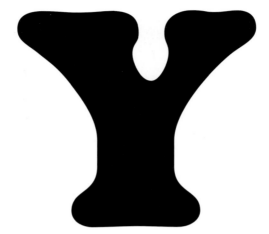

Textiles

Template for Toy Sack

1 2 3

4 5 6

7 8 9

Template for Toy Sack

Leftovers

Leftovers

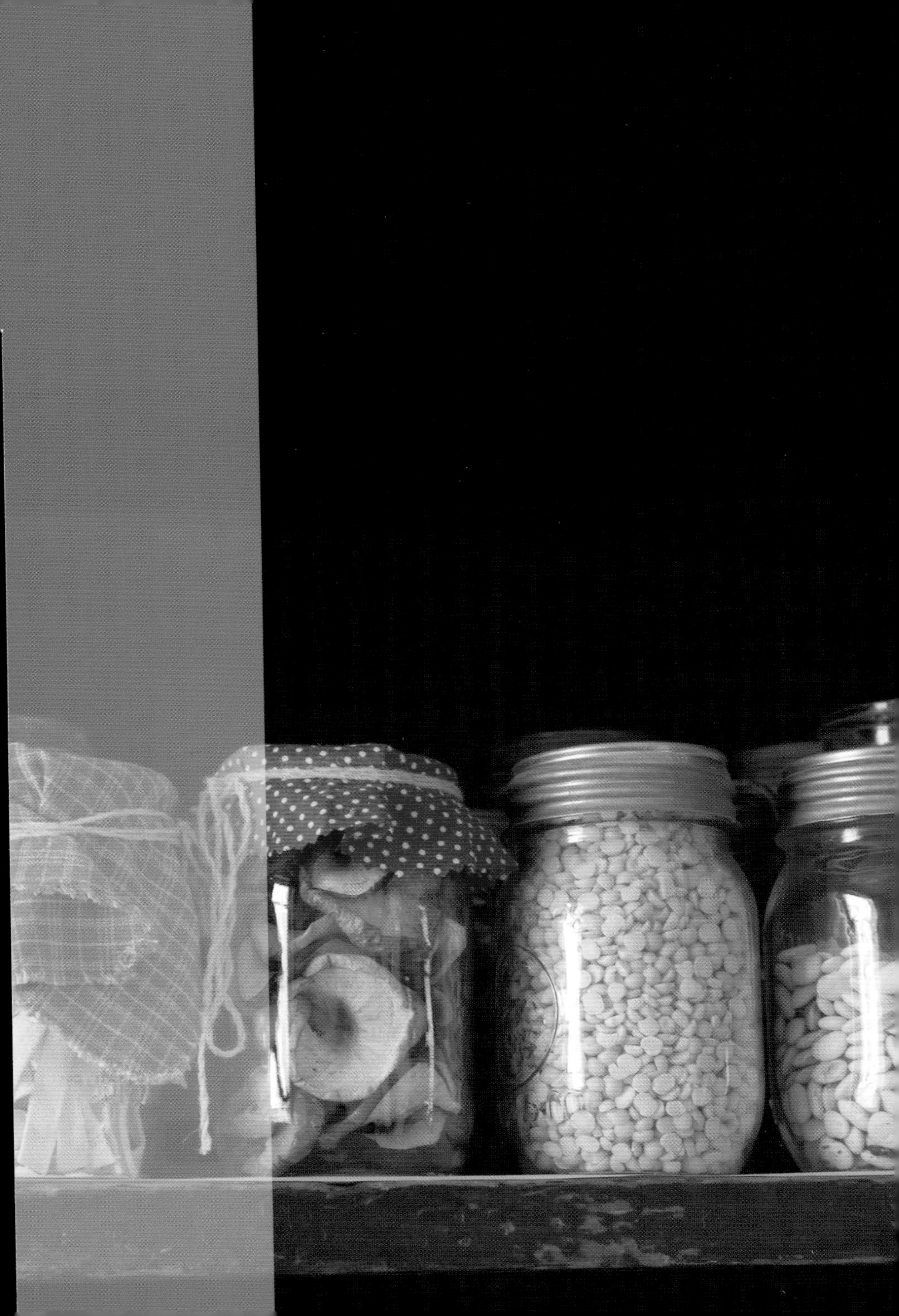

Food Waste

Probably the single biggest area of waste in your home is in the kitchen. Recent statistics show that a shockingly large amount of food is thrown away, and it's not just leftovers. We have all been guilty of throwing away food when we have overbought. "Use by" dates creep up on us and before you know it, our bins are overflowing with food that hasn't even been taken out of its packaging.

Wasting food is not only a waste of money, but also creates environmental issues. You can cut down on wasting food with some simple tips:

Plan your meals - use a shopping list!

As much as you can try and plan ahead your meals. Think about the vegetables that you will be using and how long their shelf life is. There is no point buying huge amounts of say broccoli thinking that you are going to use it every day. By day 3 you will be fed up with broccoli and by the time you go to use the remainder of it, the likelihood is that it will have gone past it best. The best way to plan ahead is to use a shopping list!

Storage

Storing food correctly can give it added shelf life. Invaluable tools in the battle against kitchen waste are:

Airtight jars
These keep dry foods fresher longer.

Airtight box containers
With well fitted lids these can be used for keeping fresh pretty much everything in your fridge including cheese, cooked meats, bacon, sausages etc.

Bread Bags
Invest in a cloth bread bag which will give your bread extra shelf life.

Blender
A great way of using excess fruit or vegetables is to blend into smoothies or soups.

Clingfilm
Cover leftovers with clingfilm before storing in the fridge. Use a permanent marker pen to write the date on the clingfilm so you know how long it's been in the fridge.

Fridge
Generally storing foods in the fridge will keep them fresher for longer, but make sure that your fridge is kept clean, organised and at the right temperature which should be between 1º - 5ºC.

Freezer
If you've something in your fridge that it doesn't look like you are going to use before it's "use by" date check and see if it can be frozen. If not, check and see if there is any other food that you can freeze and swap around your meals accordingly. If when you are cooking you end up with too much of something that you don't want to use immediately, store in a container or freezer bag for future use.

Weights and Measures
Portion control is paramount in controlling food waste so make sure you have a good set of measuring spoons/jugs and scales. Follow the recommended allowance on packets - even if it does seem slightly small - because it is better to make more or fill up on something else than throw away food which is surplus to requirements.

Leftover foods are cooked foods that you or your family do not eat within 2 hours after they are cooked. Leftovers include foods that you may eat before or after they have been stored in the refrigerator or freezer. The chance of food poisoning increases the longer you store a food after it is cooked. Improper handling or storing cooked food is one of the most common causes of food poisoning in the home which is why it is important to mark your leftovers with the date before storing.

You can also reduce the threat of food poisoning by following the guidelines below for storing, reheating, and disposing of leftover foods.

Storing Leftovers

All cooked foods should be reheated to 165° F, refrigerated, or frozen within 2 hours after cooking. In hot weather, that time limit is only 1 hour. Remember that the "safe" period starts after the food is cooked. It includes the time that the food sits before being served and the time it sits on the table while the meal is being eaten. This period lasts until the food is actually in the refrigerator or freezer.

Remember to wash your hands with soap and water before handling any cooked food, especially food you store to eat later. Use clean utensils to handle the food, and store it in clean containers. Do not put food back into the same container it was in before it was cooked, unless you have carefully cleaned the container with soap and water. Do not place food on a counter or cutting board before refrigerating or freezing, unless you have carefully cleaned the surface beforehand.

You should place foods to be refrigerated or frozen in small, shallow containers, 3 inches tall or less, and cover them completely. Don't stack these containers right next to other containers, but leave some air space around them. By using shallow containers and by leaving air space around the containers you can promote rapid, even cooling of the food. When you refrigerate or freeze cooked food in a large, deep container, the food in the centre of the container remains warm for a longer time. Dangerous bacteria may grow in this warm spot without making the food look or smell bad. If you eat this food later, you may get food poisoning. Never taste leftovers that are of questionable age or safety.

As a general rule, never keep leftovers for more than 4 days.

Remember to remove the stuffing from cooked poultry and refrigerate or freeze it separately. You should do this because the stuffing in the centre of the bird can stay warm long enough for food poisoning bacteria to grow. By removing the stuffing and placing it in its own container, you allow it to cool more rapidly. If you date leftovers before refrigerating them, this can help you ensure they don't remain in your refrigerator too long.

Warming Leftover Foods

When leftover foods are reheated, make sure you heat them completely. Leftovers that are merely "warmed" and not heated throughout are much more likely to cause food poisoning. Cover any leftover sauces, soups, gravies, and other "wet" foods, and heat them to a rolling boil before they are served. Heat all other foods to 165° F throughout. Be sure to stir foods while you reheat them, to ensure that all the food reaches the appropriate temperature.

Throwing Away Leftovers

When leftovers have been in the refrigerator too long or if they look or smell unusual, throw them out! Anytime you are in doubt about the freshness or safety of any food, dispose of it. This is especially important for leftover foods. Dispose of any potentially unsafe food in a garbage disposal or a tightly wrapped package, so that it cannot be eaten by other people or animals.

If you follow these suggestions for handling leftover foods safely, you will improve the safety of your family's food. Food poisoning is a preventable tragedy, and you can prevent it by following these simple guidelines for handling leftovers safely.

Bubble and squeak

Ingredients:
1 tablespoon butter
1/2 onion, finely chopped
handful of any cooked green vegetables
110g/4oz mashed potato
salt and freshly ground black pepper
1 tablespoon olive oil

Instructions:
Heat the butter in a frying pan and gently fry the onion and greens until softened.

Place the mashed potato in a bowl. and add the onions and vegetable mix and season well with salt and freshly ground black pepper, then mix well.

Using your hands, shape the mixture into a patty. Heat the oil in a frying pan and fry the patty, turning once, until golden-brown all over.

Chicken Nachos Recipe

Ingredients:
1 large bag of nacho chips
1 can refried beans
450ml/2 cups grated cheddar cheese
450ml/2 cups cooked chicken,
chopped
1 large jar salsa

Instructions:
Line a baking
sheet with foil
and spread the
chips evenly on

the sheet. Drop small spoonfuls of refried beans on the chips.

Mix together the salsa and chicken then spoon the mixture evenly over the chips. Top with cheddar cheese and bake in a medium oven for 8 to 12 minutes, or until the cheese is fully melted.

Chinese Chicken Salad

Ingredients:
110-170g/4-6 oz cooked chicken, diced
2 Tablespoons of soy sauce
75ml/1/3 cups honey mustard salad dressing
1/2 head iceberg lettuce, shredded
1 carrot, peeled and shredded
3 spring onions thinly sliced
115ml/1/2 cup crunchy chow mein noodles

Instructions:
Toss the chicken with 2 tablespoons of soy sauce and then mix together the lettuce carrots and mustard salad dressing. Top with chow mein noodles and spring onions.

Corned Beef Hash

Ingredients:
4 boiled potatoes, diced into cubes
3 tablespoons olive oil
1 onion, finely diced
1 garlic clove, crushed
340g/12oz corned beef, tinned
salt and freshly ground black pepper, to taste
1 tablespoon vinegar
2 free-range eggs (per person)
tomato ketchup, to serve (optional)

Instructions:
Heat a frying pan until hot. Add one tablespoon of the olive oil, the onion

and garlic and fry for two to three minutes.

Add the potatoes and fry for a further minute then crumble in the corned beef and mix together.

Bring a pan of water to the boil, add the vinegar and whirl the water around. Crack an egg into a ladle then pour the egg into the pan and simmer for two minutes, until ready. Remove from the pan and drain.

Spoon the corned beef hash into individual sized serving bowls then place under the grill for three to four minutes, until crusty.

Remove the hash from the grill and top with the egg. Top with a squeeze of ketchup if desired.

Crispy Potato Patties Recipe

Ingredients:
450ml/2 cups mashed potatoes
1 egg, beaten
1 onion, minced
1/4 teaspoon salt
1/8 teaspoon white pepper
2-3 tablespoons olive oil

Instructions:
Mix together mashed potatoes, beaten egg and onion in a medium bowl. Add salt and pepper and stir.

Over medium heat, heat olive oil in a medium size nonstick frying pan.

Drop about 110ml/1/4 cup of the potato mixture into the frying pan, patting it into 10cm/4 inch circles that are 2cm/1/2" thick.

Cook until bottom is browned and crisp, about 3-4 minutes. Carefully turn the patty over and cook the second side until brown and crisp, 3-4 minutes.

Fish Pie with Béchamel Sauce

Ingredients:
300g/1/2lb of any cooked fish
375ml/1 2/3 cups milk
1 small onion, roughly chopped
1 medium carrot, roughly chopped
1 stalk celery, roughly chopped
Leftover mashed potatoes for topping
a few peppercorns
25g/1oz butter (plus butter for greasing dish and top of pie)
25g/1oz plain flour
salt and freshly ground black pepper

Instructions:
Heat the oven to 200C/400F/Gas Mark 6 and place the fish (flaked), onion, carrot, celery and peppercorns in the bottom of a buttered ovenproof dish.

Make the béchamel sauce by melting 1oz butter over a low to medium heat then add the flour and stir well with a wooden spoon to make a roux.

Cook for two minutes, stirring every few seconds. Then gently whisk in one third of the milk. The paste will quickly turn into a very thick sauce.

Add another third of the milk, whisking all the time, and then the final third, so you end up with a creamy sauce. Season the béchamel with salt and freshly ground black pepper, turn the heat down to very low, and let the sauce bubble gently for five minutes.

Pour the sauce over the fish in the dish, mixing thoroughly so that the fish is fully coated. Spoon over the mash and spread it carefully across the surface of the fish sauce.

Dot a little extra butter over the top of the pie. Bake for about 25 minutes or until the top is starting to brown.

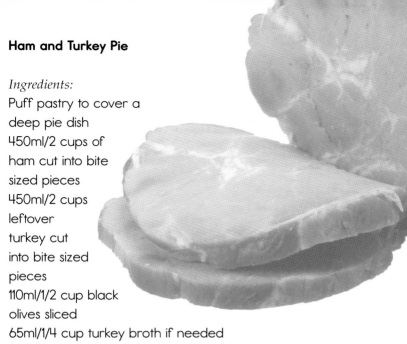

Ham and Turkey Pie

Ingredients:
Puff pastry to cover a
deep pie dish
450ml/2 cups of
ham cut into bite
sized pieces
450ml/2 cups
leftover
turkey cut
into bite sized
pieces
110ml/1/2 cup black
olives sliced
65ml/1/4 cup turkey broth if needed
Celery salt
Grated nutmeg
Salt and pepper
Butter as needed

Instructions:
Preheat your oven to 200°C/400°F/Gas Mark 6. Place a layer of turkey in the pie pan and season with celery salt, nutmeg, salt, and pepper.

Add a few dabs of butter and a handful of ham. Sprinkle some olives over the layer and season as before. Add another layer of turkey, season and add then turkey broth.

Fit the pastry over the pie dish, crimping the pastry over the edge of the pie dish then cut some holes into the top of the pie to let out the steam.

Bake for 15 minutes or until the pastry is golden brown.

You can substitute the turkey with chicken or any other poultry.

Leftovers

Homestyle Hashbrowns

Ingredients:
200g/7 oz leftover roast or boiled potatoes cut into bite-sized chunks
1 onion, finely chopped
2 tablespoons Olive oil
Butter
Salt and pepper to season

Instructions:
Heat the oil and butter in a non-stick frying pan and add the onions. Cook until soft then add the potatoes and cook until golden brown.

Season with salt and pepper.

You can always try adding fresh herbs or other favourite spices for a kick. If you prefer a sweeter taste, try adding a good pinch of brown sugar or a teaspoon of honey.

These hash browns taste great with both breakfast, lunch and dinner ingredients. Try them with grilled bacon and soft poached eggs for breakfast or with grilled fish or beef stew for dinner.

Italian Beef Rolls

Ingredients:
1 onion, chopped
1 tablespoon olive oil
3 cups leftover mashed potatoes
2 tablespoon milk
8 slices cooked roast beef
400g/14 oz can diced tomatoes with garlic, undrained
225g/8 oz can tomato passata sauce
1/2 teaspoon dried basil leaves
1/2 teaspoon salt
1/8 teaspoon pepper
225ml/1 cup grated Parmesan cheese

Instructions:
Preheat oven to 180°C/350°F/Gas Mark 4.

In a small saucepan, sauté onion in olive oil until tender. Stir onions into potatoes, along with milk and 110ml/1/2 cup Parmesan cheese. Divide the potato mixture among roast beef slices.

Roll up to enclose the potato mixture. Pour 2 tablespoons of tomato sauce in bottom of large glass baking dish, spread to cover thinly. Place beef rolls in pan, seam side down.

Mix diced tomatoes, remaining tomato sauce, basil, salt, and pepper and pour over filled rolls.

Cover pan with foil and then bake at 180°C/350°F/Gas Mark 4 for 25-30 minutes, until bubbly. Uncover pan and sprinkle with 1/2 cup Parmesan cheese. Bake 5 minutes longer until cheese melts.

Plum Duck Salad

Ingredients:
110ml/175ml/4-6 oz cooked duck, diced
2 tablespoons of plum sauce
75ml/1/3 cup honey mustard salad dressing
1/2 head iceberg lettuce, shredded
1 carrot, peeled and shredded
3 spring onions thinly sliced
110ml/1/2 cup crunchy chow mein noodles

Instructions:
Toss the duck with 2 tablespoons of plum sauce and then mix together the lettuce carrots and mustard salad dressing. Top with chow mein noodles and spring onions.

Potato and Bacon omelette
The omelette is the classic left over dish as other than fresh eggs, you can pretty much use anything you have.

Ingredients:
1 medium onion, finely chopped
4 slices of bacon, chopped
Leftover potato
Olive oil
6 beaten eggs
25g/1oz butter
125g/4oz left over cheese

Instructions:
Preheat the grill. Heat a non-stick frying pan with a splash of olive oil and a knob of butter.

Cook a chopped onion with a little bacon for 3-4 minutes or until lightly golden then add the left over chopped potato and cook until lightly golden.

Whisk the eggs together and pour over the potatoes with the crumbled or grated cheese. Cook over the heat until the egg begins to set. Finish it off under a hot grill until the centre is set and the omelette light brown.

Pumpkin

Many of us carve pumpkins at halloween so here are a few recipes to ensure you don't waste the scooped out pumpkin flesh and seeds.

Pumpkin Pasta

Ingredients:
340g/12oz pasta such as conchiglie (large shells)
1 small pumpkin
1 clove garlic
1 shallot
140ml/5fl oz carton double cream
1 teaspoon Dijon mustard
30-55g/1-2oz butter
150ml/¼ pint white wine
1/2 lemon, juice only
salt and freshly ground black pepper
grated parmesan, to serve

Instructions:
Preheat the oven 190C/375F/Gas Mark 5. Dice the pumpkin into 2.5cm/1in cubes and place onto an ovenproof sheet. Season with salt and pepper and drizzle with olive oil then place in the oven and cook for 45 minutes.

Cook the pasta and chop the garlic and shallot then gently pan-fry in the butter for about 1 minute. Add the mustard and wine then bring to the boil and simmer for 2-3 minutes.

Add the lemon juice, seasoning and cream. Drain the pasta and mix with the pumpkin in a large serving bowl then pour over the sauce and mix thoroughly. Serve with grated parmesan cheese.

Pumpkin Pie

Ingredients:
Sweet short crust pastry case
450 g/1lb prepared weight pumpkin flesh, cut into 1in/2.5 cm chunks
2 large eggs plus 1 yolk (use the white for another dish)
75g/3 oz soft dark brown sugar
1 teaspoon ground cinnamon
1/2 level teaspoon freshly grated nutmeg
1/2 teaspoon ground allspice
1/2 teaspoon ground cloves
1/2 teaspoon ground ginger
275 ml/10 fl oz double cream

Instructions:
Pre-heat the oven to 180C/350F/Gas Mark 4. Use a shop bought sweet crust pastry case, about 23 cm/9 inch diameter and 1½ inches/4 cm deep.

Steam the pumpkin then place in a coarse sieve and press lightly to extract any excess water. Lightly whisk the eggs and extra yolk together in a large bowl. Mix the sugar, spices and the cream in a pan, bring to simmering point, mix everything together then pour it over the eggs and whisk again. Add the pumpkin, still whisking to combine everything thoroughly. Pour the filling into your pastry case and bake for 35-40 minutes.

Roast Pumpkin Seeds

Ingredients:
100g/3½oz pumpkin seeds
1/4 teaspoon celery salt
1/4 teaspoon salt
1/4 teaspoon freshly ground black pepper
1/4 teaspoon paprika
1 teaspoon vegetable oil

Instructions:
Heat a frying pan over a medium heat and brush lightly with a little oil. Add the pumpkin seeds.

They will expand and brown fairly quickly, and when this is done, place them in a bowl and add the salt, celery salt, freshly ground black pepper and paprika.

Shepherd's Pie

Ingredients:
1 small onion, peeled and chopped
300gm/11oz of cooked beef, ground or diced
salt and black pepper
225ml/1 cup of peas
225ml/1 cup of diced carrot
Gravy to taste
Left-over mash for topping
Butter

Instructions:
Preheat your oven to 180°C/350°F/Gas Mark 4. In a large skillet or frying pan over medium-high heat, saute the onion in 2 tablespoons butter and add the ground beef. Season with salt and pepper, to taste and cook until brown.

Grease a glass ovenproof dish with butter then add the beef, peas and carrots. If the mixture seems dry, add gravy to moisten but the mixture should not be too wet.

Spoon over the mash and spread it carefully across the surface covering the beef. Melt a little butter in a pan and drizzle over the top of the mash. Bake for about 25 minutes or until the top is starting to brown.

This dish can also be made with lamb.

Sweet Potato Wontons

Ingredients:
4 tablespoon butter
1 red pepper, diced
65ml/1/4 cup finely chopped onion
2 teaspoons curry powder
225ml/1 cup chopped cooked sweet potatoes
1 tablespoon flour
65ml/1/4 cup sour cream
2 tablespoons mango chutney
24 wonton squares

Instructions:
Melt 2 tablespoons of butter in a large heavy skillet, and cook the red pepper, onion and curry powder until vegetables soften and become tender.

Stir in the cooked sweet potatoes then allow to cool. Stir the flour, sour cream, and chutney into the sweet potato mixture.

Preheat oven to 180°C/350°F/Gas Mark 4. Brush the wonton squares with 2 tablespoons of melted butter and press each into a cupcake case.

Spoon sweet potato mixture into the wonton shells and bake at 350 degrees for 12-15 minutes until golden brown. Makes 24 filled wontons.

This recipe also tastes delicious with other leftovers such as potatoes or pumpkin.

Turkey Soufflé

Ingredients:
450ml/2 cups diced leftover turkey
225ml/1 cup cooked rice
225ml/1 cup soft bread crumbs
225ml/1 cup turkey stock or gravy
1 teaspoon salt
1 pinch of fresh ground pepper
2 teaspoons stuffing
1/4 teaspoon coriander
1/4 teaspoon onion salt
4 eggs separated

Instructions:
Preheat your oven to 170°C/325°F/Gas Mark 3. Wrap a large soufflé dish with a piece of white paper so that the paper is well above the edge of the dish then tape or tie the paper in place.

Mix the turkey, rice, crumbs, and the stock or gravy in a bowl until well combined then season with salt, pepper, onion salt, and coriander.

Beat the egg yolks until light and smooth and mix into the turkey mixture. Next, beat the egg whites until stiff then fold gently into the turkey mixture.

Immediately pour the mixture into the soufflé dish then place the dish into a shallow pan of hot water. Bake for one hour and 15 minutes or until well risen and firm on top. Remove paper and serve immediately.

Vegetable Quesadillas

These tasty quesadillas can be filled with virtually any leftover that you have.

Ingredients:

500g/18oz mashed cooked vegetables

8 flour tortillas

Ground Black peppercorns

Sea Salt

300g/11oz of crumbled or grated cheese (can be different varieties mixed)

Instructions:

Place a flour tortilla in a dry nonstick frying pan and lavishly spread with the mashed vegetables, right to the edges.

Season with salt and pepper and scatter with the cheese. Top with another flour tortilla and cook over a medium heat until lightly browned, about 3 minutes.

Turn once, and cook the other side until lightly browned and the cheese has melted. Cut in half or into quarters to serve.

Try substituting or adding different leftovers such as meats or fish.

Energy & Water

Water

We are all using 50% more water than 25 years ago thanks
to the increased use of washing machines and dishwashers,
people taking more baths and more people getting into gardening.

The quantity of the water we use each day can quite easily be decreased
by making a few simple changes in our day to day lives.

Here are some tips and advice on how to use water
wisely in the home and garden.

Brushing your teeth
You don't need to have the tap running while you
are brushing your teeth as it can waste as much as
5 litres of water per minute. This also applies to shaving and washing
your hands.

Dripping taps
4 litres of water can be wasted a day from a dripping tap. Get them
fixed as soon as you notice them.

Hot and Cold water
When you are running the tap to get hot water, it normally takes a few
seconds before the water becomes hot and in those few seconds
the cold water is just being wasted down the tap. Keep a bowl
in the sink to collect the cold water and use to water the
plants. The same applies when we are running the tap for
cold water to drink, it usually takes a few seconds for it to
be nice and cold. Instead of doing this keep a jug or
bottles of water in the fridge so you always have nice cold
water.

Kettle
When boiling the kettle, only boil the amount you need.

Shower
Having a five minute shower uses about a third of the water in a bath. But take note if you have a power shower, as some of these can use more than a bath in less than 5 minutes!!

Toilets
Old toilets can use up to 9 litres of clean water every time they are flushed. You can reduce this by putting a 1 Litre plastic bottle (filled with water with the lid sealed tight) or a toilet hippo in your cistern. Make sure the objects you put in do not obstruct the flushing mechanism.

Vegetables and fruit
When you are rinsing vegetables, do it in a bowl and not under a running tap and then the leftover water can be used for watering the house plants.

Washing Machines and Dishwashers
Half load programmes on washing machines and dishwashers use more than half the water and energy of a full load. Always wait until you have a full load before you switch the machine on.

Saving water in the Garden

There are many ways to save water in the garden, here are some of them.

Hose pipes

If you do need to use a hose pipe, make sure you have a trigger to control the water flow so you can turn it off when you do not need it.

Morning and Evening watering

In the summer water your plants early in the morning and late at night. This will allow the water to soak in as when the temperature goes up, a lot of the water will evaporate before it gets chance to soak in.

Water Butt

Have a water butt fitted to your downpipe. Almost 100,000 litres of rainwater falls on the average roof each year, so if you have a water butt to collect the rainwater you can use the water for your plants and lawn and even for washing your car. If you want to collect more water than one butt can hold you can buy a connector kit to link up two or more. You can usually get water butts at discounted prices from your local council.

Watering Cans

Using a watering can instead of a hose pipe can save a lot of water.

Watering your lawn

Lawns need a lot of water, but here are some ways that you can reduce the amount of water your lawn needs. In hot weather let the grass grow longer, this will help keep moisture in the soil. If you really do need to water your lawn do it infrequently as this will encourage the roots to search deeper for water. If the grass does go brown it does not necessarily mean it has died. More often than not the grass will grow again after the next rain shower.

Weeding regularly

By weeding regularly you will be watering the plants not the weeds!!

There are many ways to save energy in the house. With just a little effort you can reduce the energy used in your house and at the same time cut down on your energy bills.

Central Heating
By turning your heating down by 1°C, you can cut your heating bills down by up to 10%.

Curtains
Hang thick curtains. This will stop the heat escaping through the windows.

Draught proofing
Even tiny cracks can allow precious heat to escape – if you can feel cold air, that means warm air is escaping too. Keyholes, gaps round doors and windows and between floorboards are all culprits and can let as much as 20% of your heat escape. So plug those gaps and watch your bills plummet by around £20 a year.

You can easily fill in the gaps yourself. See page 40 for how to make draft excluders. You can also use fillers, sealants and tape which you can get from your local DIY Store.

Energy saving light bulbs
Fit energy saving light bulbs, these bulbs can save you over £100 over the lifetime of the bulb. They last up to 10 times longer than normal light bulbs and they use 25% less energy. You can now get them in all sorts of different shapes and shades.

Washing
Wash clothes at 30°C. This will reduce the energy used by nearly half.

Hot water tank
Check the temperature on your hot water tank. it should be no more than 60°C.

Insulating your loft
By insulating your loft you could save around £100 a year on your bills. As much as 15% of the heat generated in your house can be lost through your roof. Fitting loft insulation is quite easy to do. Thick insulating material can be bought from your local DIY store - the recommended thickness is 270mm. It is quite straightforward to do as you simply lay it between the joists.

Insulating your pipes and hot water tank

If you insulate your hot water tank and pipes, you'll save energy and keep your water hotter too as less heat can escape. It's great for everyone who likes hot baths and lower bills!

Turning Off!

When you leave a room always turn the light off. Never leave the TV, CD player or anything else on standby. Leaving appliances on standby uses almost as much electricity as when they are turned on. Never over charge your phone.

Reuse Tips

We hope that you have found the tips and ideas for reusing and recycling helpful and no doubt you have many ideas of your own. Please use this section to make a note of your own methods of reusing and recycling.

Reuse Tips

Reuse Tips

Index

index

Index

Index

Index

Index

Spoons to millilitres

1/2 Teaspoon	2.5ml	1 Tablespoon	15ml
1 Teaspoon	5ml	2 Tablespoons	30ml
1-1/2 Teaspoons	7.5ml	3 Tablespoon	45ml
2 Teaspoons	10 ml	4 Tablespoons	60ml

Grams to Ounces

10g	0.25oz	225g	8oz
15g	0.38oz	250g	9oz
25g	1oz	275g	10oz
50g	2oz	300g	11oz
75g	3oz	350g	12oz
110g	4oz	375g	13oz
150g	5oz	400g	14oz
175g	6oz	425g	15oz
200g	7oz	450g	16oz

Metric to Cups

Description	Metric	Cup
Flour etc	115g	1 cup
Clear Honey etc	350g	1 cup
Liquids	225ml	1 cup

Liquid measures

Fl oz	Pints	ml
5fl oz	1/4 pint	150ml
7.5fl oz		215ml
10fl oz	1/2 pint	275ml
15fl oz		425ml
20fl oz	1 pint	570ml
35fl oz	1-3/4 pints	1 litre

Temperature

Celsius	Farenheit	Gas Mark	Description
110c	225F	1/4	very cool
130c	250F	1/2	very cool
140c	275F	1	cool
150c	300F	2	cool
170c	325F	3	very moderate
180c	350F	4	moderate
190c	375F	5	moderate
200c	400F	6	moderately hot
220c	425F	7	hot
230c	450F	8	hot
240c	475F	9	very hot

Conversion Charts